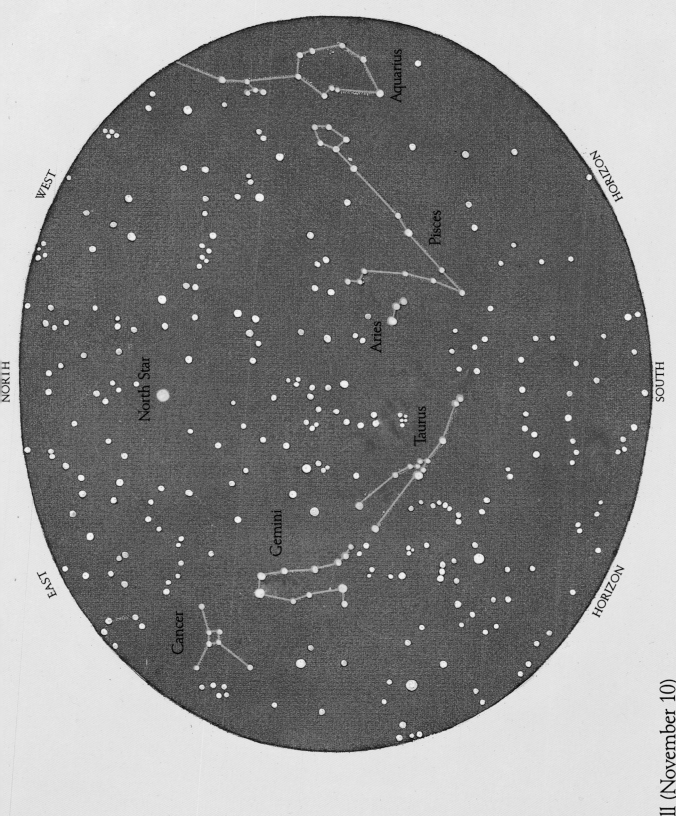

Fall (November 10)

Facing South, hold page overhead with the arrow pointing North.

In ancient times, people looked up to the sky and saw pictures in the stars. We call these pictures constellations. The constellations took the shapes of heroes and villains, lovers and foes, gods and goddesses, and a host of marvelous mythological creatures. Behind every constellation, there was a story. Why is it important to know about the constellations? For the same reason it is good to know the names of the flowers and trees and birds—because they are a part of your everyday world. Knowing the stories behind this heavenly cast of players helps you to fix them in your mind, and gives you something wonderful to talk about nights as you huddle outside, with your flashlight and glowing star charts in hand and your gaze trained upward. The people who told these stories are long dead, but the emotions the stories depict—fear, jealousy, envy, compassion, love—are as alive today as they were over two thousand years ago, when the stories were first told. These tales are our link with the ancients—and with the heavens themselves. This book will help forge that link.

Text copyright © 1993 by Random House, Inc.
Illustrations copyright © 1993 by Stephen Marchesi. All rights reserved under International and Pan-American Copyright Conventions. Published in the United States by Random House, Inc., New York, and simultaneously in Canada by Random House of Canada Limited, Toronto.
Library of Congress Catalog Card Number: 92-61555 ISBN: 0-679-82470-7
Manufactured in Taiwan 10 9 8 7 6 5 4 3 2 1

THE
GLOW·IN·THE·DARK
ZODIAC
STORYBOOK

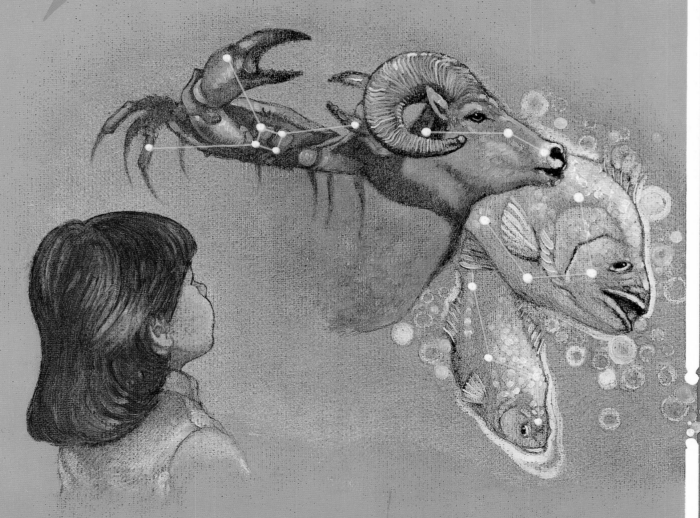

By Katharine Ross ○ Illustrated by Stephen Marchesi

Random House New York

Aries • the Ram ♈

Jason needed the golden hide of Aries, the sacred ram, in order to claim his rightful throne. He set sail aboard his ship, the *Argo,* and had many adventures before landing at last on the island of Colchis, where the fleece was said to be. King Aeëtes of Colchis did not wish to give up the fleece. His daughter, Medea, an enchantress, fell in love with Jason and promised to help him steal it. One night she led him to the dark grove where the Golden Fleece, shining like the sun, hung on the branch of a sacred oak. A never-sleeping serpent was coiled around the trunk, guarding the hide. Medea put a spell on the serpent, and it fell into a deep sleep. Jason grabbed the Golden Fleece and made off with it—and Medea —to the waiting *Argo.* Quietly, they slipped out to sea.

Taurus • the Bull ♉

Zeus visited earth in many disguises. Once he came down from Mount Olympus in the form of a fierce bull to woo the fair Europa. Europa was playing in a meadow by the sea with her handmaidens when she first saw the bull. She was terrified! Then she came closer and looked into his eyes. How gentle and kind he looked! The bull bowed down so that Europa could climb on his broad back. No sooner was she astride than away the bull galloped across the waves. "Do not fear," he whispered to Europa, "I am Zeus. And I have come to make you my bride and the queen of Crete!"

Gemini • the Twins ♊

Another time Zeus came down to earth in the form of a swan to win the heart of Leda. Their union produced twin boys, named Castor and Pollux. Castor was mortal, while Pollux was a god. They grew up with different interests. Castor was a horseman. Pollux liked to box. But they were the best of friends and went everywhere together— even to war. When they died side by side in battle, Pollux went up to Olympus, but Castor went down to Hades. They missed each other so badly that Zeus took pity on them and placed them among the stars, where they remain, together, to this day.

Cancer • the Crab 69

Zeus' wife Hera hated the brave and powerful Hercules. Out of spite, she made him go berserk. In his madness, he mistook his own children for wild animals and killed them. Grief-stricken, Hercules went to his cousin, King Eurystheus of Tiryns, who ordered him to perform twelve difficult tasks to atone for his crime. One of these tasks was to kill the Hydra, a hideous nine-headed serpent. Hercules went to the swamps of Lerna, where the Hydra lived. The mighty hero began to lop off the beast's heads. To his horror, two heads grew back for every one he chopped off. But clever Hercules used a torch to burn the stumps so that no new heads could grow. When Hera saw that Hercules was starting to win, she sent down Cancer, the giant crab. Hercules took one look at the crab, picked it up, and hurled it at the last head of the Hydra, killing both enemies in one fell swoop.

Leo • the Lion

Leo • *the Lion* ◌

Another one of Hercules' difficult tasks was to slay the Nemean lion. This lion was extremely fierce, and its hide was so tough that no weapon could pierce it. But Hercules tracked the lion to its lair and, with his bare hands, strangled it to death. Hercules skinned the lion and thereafter always wore the golden pelt as a symbol of his victory— over the lion, and over Hera as well.

Virgo • *the Virgin* ♍

The iron age was a very grim time indeed. The people of the earth, once innocent and honest, became greedy and deceitful. They chopped down the beautiful forests to build ships, and they roamed the seas in search of treasure. They mined gold and iron from the earth to fashion jewelry and weapons. Where once people had lived together in harmony, now they squabbled over land and possessions. Sons waged war against their own fathers. Fierce battles raged, soaking the earth in blood. Looking down from Mount Olympus, the gods grew disgusted and, one by one, turned their eyes away from earth. All except Astraea, whose name means "crown of stars." She alone prayed for peace. As a reward for her faith, Zeus placed her among the stars. And there she remains, forever pure, the virgin.

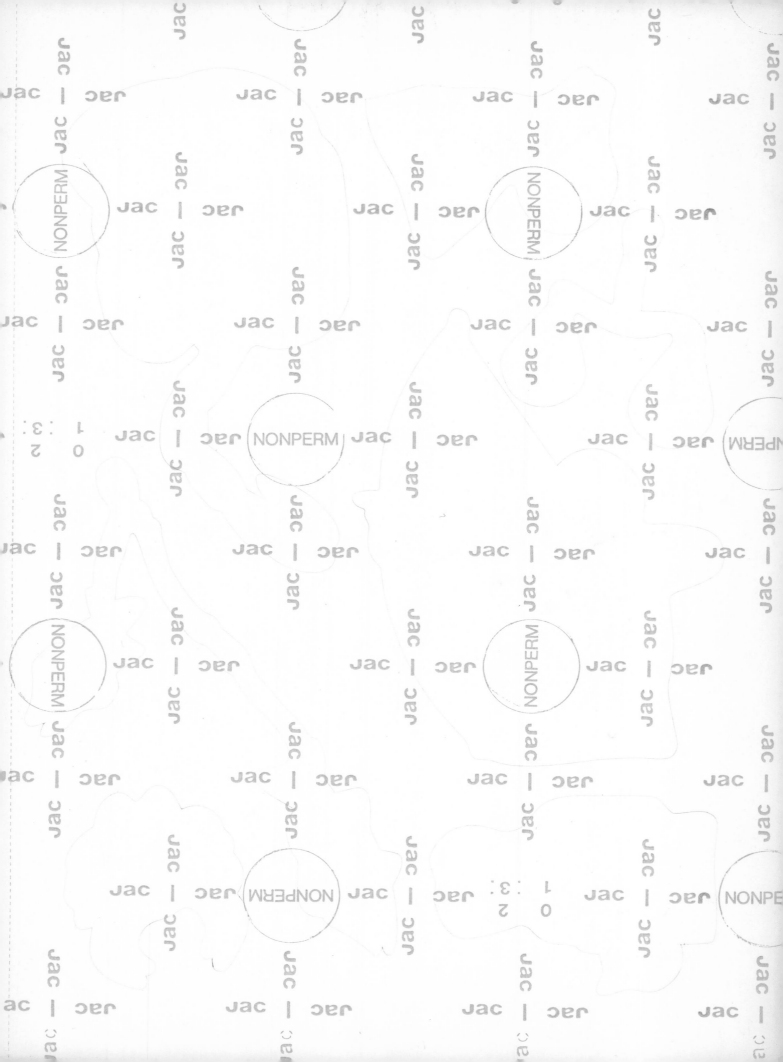

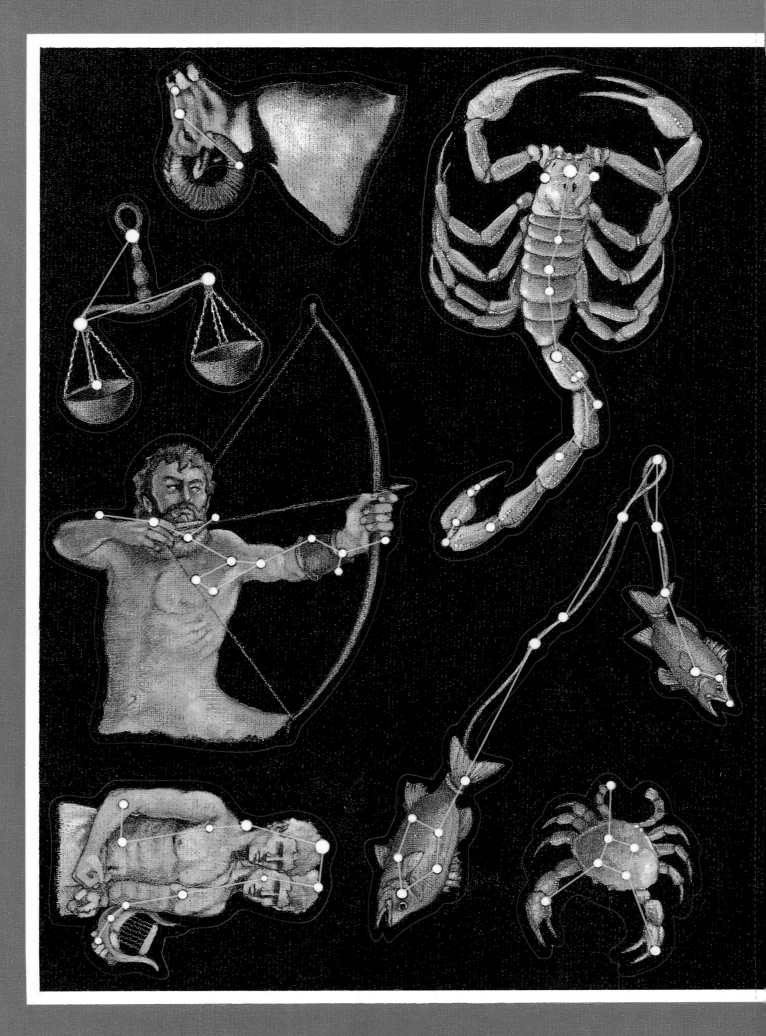

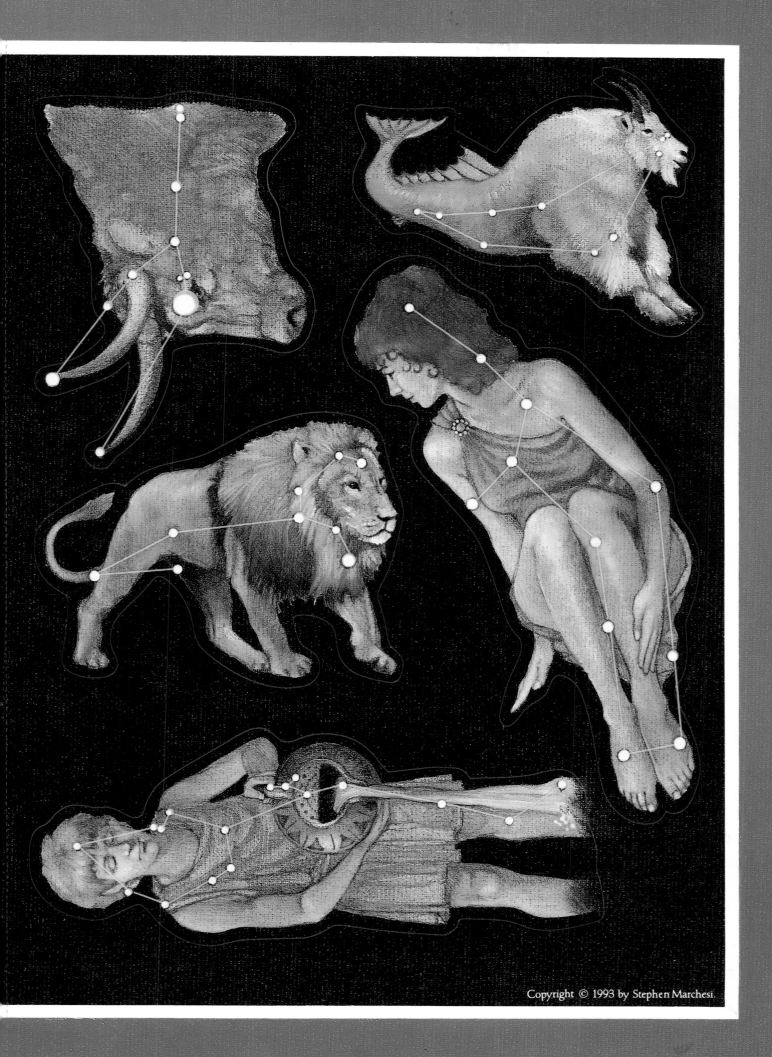

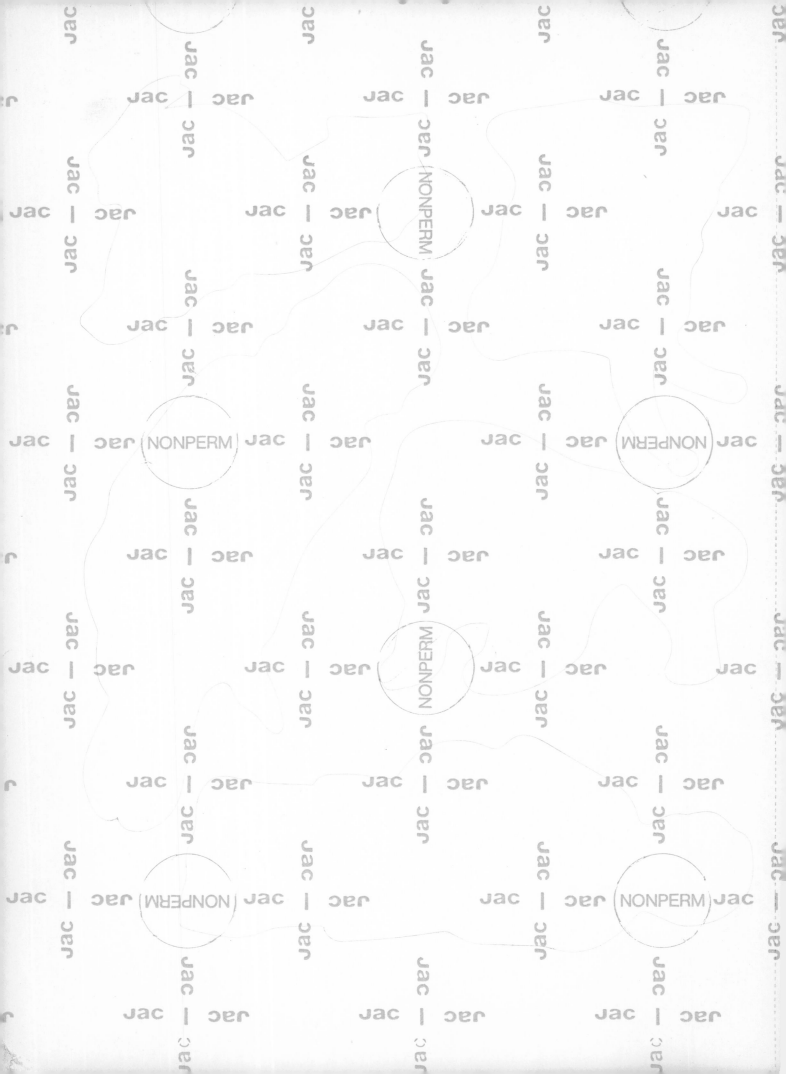

Libra • the Scales ♎

In A.D. 533, the Roman emperor Justinian I compiled the *Corpus Juris Civilis* (Body of Civil Law), a set of laws so thorough and sound that it became the basis of many modern laws. Law was the glue that held the vast Roman Empire together. The laws were written down on twelve tablets and posted in the Forum in Rome, and it was the duty of every Roman boy to memorize them. The Roman symbol for justice was a blindfolded figure holding a set of scales. The figure is blindfolded to show that the law is blind to a person's rank in life: the lowliest slave and the highest-ranking nobleman were equal under the law. To remind us that this same principle still holds today, we have only to look up at the sky at Libra, the Scales.

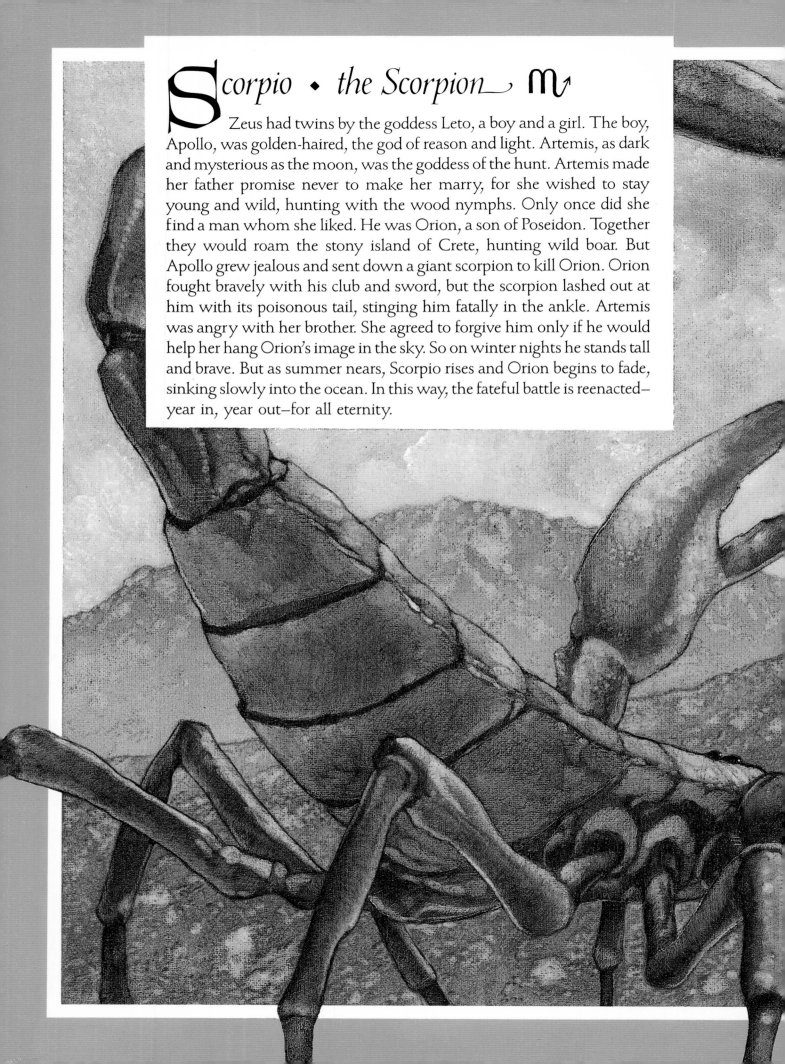

Scorpio • the Scorpion ♏︎

Zeus had twins by the goddess Leto, a boy and a girl. The boy, Apollo, was golden-haired, the god of reason and light. Artemis, as dark and mysterious as the moon, was the goddess of the hunt. Artemis made her father promise never to make her marry, for she wished to stay young and wild, hunting with the wood nymphs. Only once did she find a man whom she liked. He was Orion, a son of Poseidon. Together they would roam the stony island of Crete, hunting wild boar. But Apollo grew jealous and sent down a giant scorpion to kill Orion. Orion fought bravely with his club and sword, but the scorpion lashed out at him with its poisonous tail, stinging him fatally in the ankle. Artemis was angry with her brother. She agreed to forgive him only if he would help her hang Orion's image in the sky. So on winter nights he stands tall and brave. But as summer nears, Scorpio rises and Orion begins to fade, sinking slowly into the ocean. In this way, the fateful battle is reenacted— year in, year out—for all eternity.

Sagittarius • the Archer ♐

Half man and half horse, the centaur who appears to be aiming his arrow at Scorpio might be Chiron. It was to Chiron in his cave on Mount Pelion that kings took their sons to be taught. The wise centaur instructed his young students not only in the arts of war, archery, and swordsmanship but also in the science of healing with herbs. One of Chiron's most famous students was a son of Apollo, Asclepius, who grew up to be the first doctor in all of Greece.

Capricorn • the Goat ♑

With the head and forelegs of a goat and the tail of a fish, Capricorn lived in the ocean along with the other children of Neptune, god of the sea. Sailors of ancient Rome believed that it was Capricorn who stirred up the water to bring on rain and ocean storms.

Aquarius • the Waterbearer ≈

For some time, Zeus had been admiring from afar the handsome Trojan youth Ganymede. One day, Zeus turned himself into an eagle, swooped down, and captured the boy. Carrying Ganymede back to Olympus, the home of the gods, Zeus made him the official cupbearer to the gods. Henceforth, it was Ganymede's job to pour sweet nectar into the twelve golden goblets of the Olympian gods and goddesses.

Pisces • the Fishes ♓

One day Aphrodite, the goddess of love, was out walking with her young son, Eros, when they came upon a horrid beast. With one hundred heads, each head spewing fire and molten lava, this creature, called the Typhon, was an enemy of Zeus and all the gods and goddesses. Aphrodite and her boy ran from the monster. Just as mother and son could feel its fiery breath on their necks, they came to a river. As if by magic, two giant fish reared out of the water. Aphrodite and Eros hopped on the fishes' backs and rode downstream to safety!

Winter (February 15)

Creation with Flowers

Creation with Flowers

The Ohara School of

Japanese Flower Arrangement

by HŌUN OHARA

Published by
KODANSHA INTERNATIONAL LTD.
Tokyo, Japan & Palo Alto, Calif., U.S.A.

DISTRIBUTORS:

British Commonwealth (excluding Canada and the Far East)
WARD LOCK & COMPANY LTD.
London

France
HACHETTE—LIBRAIRIE ETRANGERE
Paris

Continental Europe (excluding France)
BOXERBOOKS, INC.
Zurich

The Far East
JAPAN PUBLICATIONS TRADING COMPANY
C.P.O. Box 722, Tokyo

Published by KODANSHA INTERNATIONAL LTD., 3-19 Otowa-cho, Bunkyo-ku, Tokyo, Japan and KODANSHA INTERNATIONAL/USA, LTD., 577 College Avenue, Palo Alto, California 94306. Copyright © 1966 by Kodansha International Ltd. All rights reserved. Printed in Japan.

Library of Congress Catalog Card No. 66-28571

First edition, 1966

Table of Contents

Preface

I have made several journeys abroad to well-known places in Europe, the United States, Central and South America for flower-arrangement demonstrations and exhibitions, and through the medium of ikebana I have made many personal friends. All of these friends and acquaintances have expressed a desire for a book combining both instruction in and appreciation of ikebana. I myself own several books on ikebana written in languages other than Japanese, but none of them combines appreciation with guidance. Just at the time I had made up my mind to write such a book, Kodansha International unexpectedly expressed a desire to publish such a book which would also include representative works of leading members of the Ohara School. That is to say, a book which would introduce Ohara ikebana in full portrait. As headmaster of the school, I expressed great approval.

Ohara Ikebana was born in the middle of the Meiji era, at the time when Japan was attempting to begin national modernization. At this time, many flowers were imported to Japan from foreign countries; but until then there had been no way to arrange these beautiful flowers. My grandfather, Unshin Ohara, having been a sculptor, arranged them in a basin he had designed and made himself; this was the beginning of modern flower arrangement. The Ohara School, from its founder Unshin through Kōun to Hōun, has continued some eighty-odd years, forming the tradition of modern ikebana, progressively refining as it developed.

After the second world war, I made great efforts toward transmitting the heart and beauty and sentiment of peace to the war-weary hearts of men through the medium of ikebana. At that time, however, there were few suitable plants available in this war-ravaged land. I made ikebana from steel and bits of broken glass, and weeds growing by the roadside. This was a discovery of new materials which led to the broadening of ikebana, the advance of the avant-garde which used materials other than fresh plants. The ikebana which my friends and I had thought to be only a matter of personal interest became known as "modern ikebana," on a level with the other modern arts.

Ohara Ikebana is a school in which both traditional styles and the most modern styles have the same basis in theory; to be able to introduce the art and methods of the Ohara School now is a great pleasure for me.

Kodansha International, publisher of this book, already has established itself as a leading Japanese publisher of books for distribution overseas. Through this book I look forward to meeting once again my friends throughout the world.

Spring 1966

HŌUN OHARA
Headmaster, Ohara School

Introduction

COLOR SCHEME ARRANGEMENT (SHIKISAI SŌKA)

The "Color Scheme" arrangement, as its name implies, uses principally plants and flowers of high coloration. Contrast and harmony of color and form become the main intent of both creation and appreciation.

There are two varieties of Color Scheme arrangement, classified from the standpoint of design principles: the Realistic and the Non-realistic.

The Realistic utilizes the natural forms of flower materials and derives hints and inspiration from the natural environment of the plant. Beauty of color is achieved in a realistic manner.

The Non-realistic, without destroying the innate character of seasonality of flowers, uses them in more contrived ways, such as in large bunches or masses, bending or wrapping stems and branches, or in combination with artificial or artificially colored flower material. (We refer to this kind of man-made plant material as "non-real.")

LANDSCAPE ARRANGEMENT (SHAKEI SŌKA)

The Landscape arrangement, with its theme of creating seasons and scenes of nature in imitation of natural beauty, is an expression of selected flowers and containers appropriate to a certain scene.

Landscape arrangements are also classified according to design principles: the Traditional and the Interpretive.

The Traditional arrangement is based on rules of formal expression: the arrangement of foliage (the placement of leaves and flowers, methods of patterning, size and length), and the ways of representing perspective distance, middle ground and foreground.

Interpretive arrangements are not merely the expression of scenery as it is, but involve the appreciation of themes introduced into the work by the individual's subjective impressions. The introduction of non-realism and "non-real" materials is a recognized technique of Interpretive arrangements.

RIMPA (CLASSICAL PAINTING SCHOOL) TONE ARRANGEMENT

In the history of painting in Japan, one school approached stylistic beauty in a particularly splendid way. This was the Rimpa school founded by Kōrin Ogata. From the beginning to the middle of the Edo period (1615–1867), the Rimpa school managed to establish a brilliant style not only in painting, but in the fields of lacquer ware, pottery, kimono and fan design.

The elegant and decorative folding screen paintings of Kōrin and his followers form the inspiration for the Ohara School's Rimpa ikebana. From the standpoint of arrangement style, it can be said that flower materials are consciously patterned in order to emphasize the decorative aspect of color and form in the arrangement.

BUNJIN (LITERARY ARTIST) TONE ARRANGEMENT

The *Bunjin* (literary artist) ikebana is the present-day reappearance of the style attributed to painters and poets of the Edo period.

Bunjin arrangements have an overwhelmingly Chinese flavor, full of zest, expressing an interest more in flowers as personalities than in ikebana itself; indeed these arrangements often tend to make fun of floral dignity.

In modern ikebana, this characteristic Chinese exoticism is represented by the use of very few flowers and striking curves in branch and leaf formation.

SHOHINKA (SMALL FLOWER ARRANGEMENT)

Shohinka means small and freely arranged flowers. Blooms of either one or two varieties, very few in number, are the characteristic of this type of arrangement. Being of a free style, the originality of the artist is brought into play, but unless the natural form and beauty of the flower materials is well appreciated, the arrangement will appear to be nothing more than sparse; for this reason it is a somewhat difficult style. As this kind of small arrangement must be balanced according to the place decorated, careful thought is required in matching the design to the surroundings. It is, nevertheless, a small ikebana that almost anyone can do, and is thus very popular.

Moribana containers, though basically no more than objects in which to place flowers, determine the variety and form of the arrangement to the extent that they are of primary importance to ikebana art.

For example, in using a compote such as in Fig. 4, since the type of container was originally a bowl for sweetened fruit, an arrangement will never attain the wide scenic expression of fields and hills no matter how hard you try. The previously explained floral forms are, of course, determined largely by the materials used, but are also limited by the container. Because of this, no matter how well one learns the mechanics of the various forms, unless one can harmonize them according to container, mastery of ikebana cannot be achieved. The beauty of a carefully arranged work is often meaningless because it does not fit the container. Ohara *moribana*, as previously stated, is divided into the two main categories of Color Scheme and Landscape arrangements; the containers themselves must also be selected in accordance with these categories.

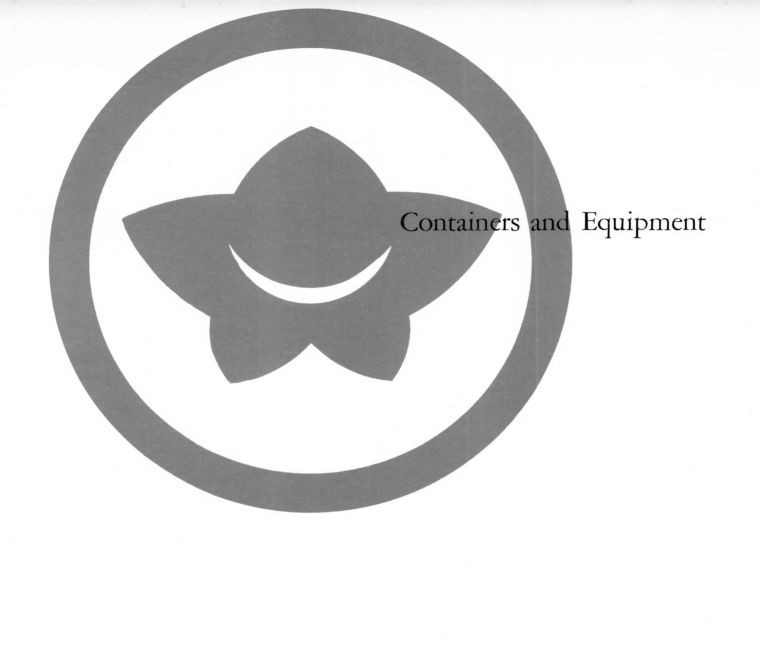

Containers and Equipment

Moribana

To The Beginner

The round flat bowl shown (7) is the standard shape used by the Ohara School, but the smallness of the semi-circular flat bowl (8) makes it particularly suitable to modern living and to the small arrangements of beginners. In proportion to one's ability to arrange standard forms in this "*moribana* standard container," one is able to progress to arrangements in keeping with the more unconventional containers.

Containers for Color Scheme Arrangements

Since the main object of the Color Scheme arrangement is the expression of pattern through color, there are many types of containers which may be used. In the range of shapes from the compote (4) to the boat-shaped one (1), the cloud-shaped one (6) and the new shapes (2, 3, and 5), color, shape and pattern must be selected and used with great skill and care.

Containers for Landscape Arrangements

As already pointed out, Landscape arrangements are devoted primarily to the representation of perspective distance, middle ground, and scenes in which water is an important element. In keeping with such themes, you should select containers which lend themselves to creating a sense of perspective—shallow vessels which are round (7) or rectangular and can be used to produce the effect of a wide expanse of water.

In its decoration the container should be relatively simple and quiet, for one which is bright or highly patterned will distract from the beauty of a Landscape arrangement.

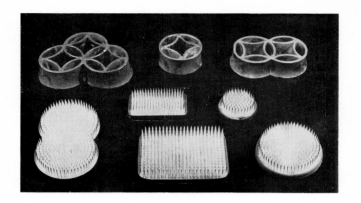

EQUIPMENT USED FOR *Moribana*

Shippō and *kenzan* are used to secure the materials used in *moribana*. There are three types of *shippō*: single, double and triple. These are used individually or in combination, depending on the quantity of materials used in the arrangement. A mass of pins face upwards in a *kenzan*, making it relatively easy to secure branches. The *kenzan* is fast replacing the *shippō* in popularity. There are round, rectangular, and moon-shaped *kenzan* in various sizes. These are used in accordance with the shape and size of the container and the materials.

Scissors with a curled end are most practical. They make it easy to determine the spot you want to cut, and the grip is such that it is easy to apply strength when cutting a comparatively thick branch.

Other tools used in ikebana are a small saw, small hand-axe, knife, and water pump.

Moribana TECHNIQUES

There are many ways to arrange flowers using the *shippō* and *kenzan*. The *shippō* and the *kenzan* have their respective advantages and disadvantages, and it is most important to recognize their characteristics in order to master the tricks of using them skillfully.

To USE THE *Shippō*

When using the *shippō* base to secure an arrangement, prop and wedge sticks must be prepared. The cut-off portions or trimmings from main branches and stalks can be used to make round supports; semi-rounds are prepared by splitting

 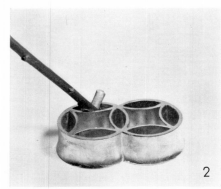  

the branch or stem in half lengthwise.

1. To stand a branch vertically upright (Fig. 1):
Usually a small opening of the *shippō* is used; supports are inserted to both left and right of the branch in order to wedge it in an upright position.

2. To stand a branch at an angle:

  a. When the branch is quite thick, and the end is cut at the proper angle, it can be fixed in place by simply inserting it into the large opening.

  b. Also common is the technique of wedging a semi-round support so that its cut side is against the main branch, at an angle opposite that of the main branch (Fig. 2).

  c. When placing a branch in a large opening, the angle can be adjusted by positioning the supports (Fig. 3).

  d. There is also the technique of inserting a support to one side of the branch in order to place it at the desired angle (Fig. 4).

3. Special ways of placement:
In the case of flowering and slender-stalked plants whose stems are thin, the stem ends can be bent upward when inserting in the *shippō*, as in Fig. 5.

4. When many flowers are used:
When many flowers and heavy branches are to be used in an arrangement, the very weight of the branches themselves may cause the arrangement to topple if only one *shippō* is used. In such cases, two *shippō* can be tied together as illustrated in Fig. 6 in order to anchor the arrangement satisfactorily.

16

5

6

7

To Use The *Kenzan*

1. To secure upright branches:

When branches are to be anchored vertically in the *kenzan*, the ends may be cut in two or three places with clippers and split before securing.

2. To secure branches at an angle:

When securing branches at an angle, cut the end at a sharp angle, then insert it in an upright position before adjusting it to the desired incline. The angle of the cut end should be facing up, opposite the direction in which the branch is inclined, as in Fig. 7.

3. Securing stemmed flowers:

When securing stemmed flowers, the stem end should be cut off at right angles before insertion. In the case of flowers like the amaryllis and calla lily, when the stem is soft and tubular, it is advisable to insert a separate stick into the opening or to place several supports around the stem in order not to damage the stem end (see Fig. 8).

4. Securing thin-stemmed flowers:

In the case of thin-stemmed flowers like the sweet pea and freesia, with stems so small they are hard to secure because of the relatively large space between the needles of the *kenzan*, either place several support sticks surrounding the stem before insertion as in Fig. 9, or insert the small stem into a cut piece of a larger one.

8

9

Heika

It is of the utmost importance in *heika* arrangement, as in *moribana*, to select a container which will complement the flowers and become a part of them. It is particularly important in choosing a *heika* container to keep in mind the characteristic elegance and refined taste of the *heika* type of arrangement.

Whether you find inspiration in a vase and then choose your flowers or select the vase according to the flowers available, *heika* ikebana is born from this harmony between flowers and container.

In the photograph below, many types of *heika* vases are shown; in Ohara, types 1 and 2 are called the "standard *nage-ire* vases." The flatness of the opening permits ease in both horizontal and vertical manipulation, and the three horizontal ridges on the sides provide places in which to conveniently lodge the ends of branches. In studying *heika*, just as in *moribana*, one must first learn to arrange flowers in the "Ohara standard *nage-ire* vase" as basic training before going on to free styles.

HEIKA TECHNIQUES

In *heika*, unlike *moribana*, flower holders are not used; the branches are supported by bracing against the sides and bottom of the vase itself. Because of this, branches merely cut off and thrown into a vase will not ordinarily stay in place, making *heika* perhaps more difficult to arrange than *moribana*. As the techniques have been evolved in a highly rational manner, however, I encourage you to master the basic principles well.

In *heika* also, both round and half-split support sticks must be prepared from the trimmings of branches and sturdy stems, but they should be left longer than those used in *moribana*.

1. To stand a branch upright (Fig. 1):

In order to stand a branch upright, it must be of sufficient length to firmly touch the bottom of the vase. When the desired branch is not long enough, a second section of branch may be tied to the first as long as it does not show above the vase rim. However, as this type of device tends to be rather unstable, it is best to either bend the branch at right angles one or two inches from the bottom end, or to split the end and insert a separate branch piece at right angles. In the latter case, the support stick ought to have been split in two so that the flat side faces downward in the vase bottom to stablize the arrangement.

2. Crosspiece holding (Figs. 2A and 2B):

When branches are to be placed at an angle, crosspieces must be used to hold them in position. When the branch is sappy and a split caused by insertion of clippers will not extend far up the stem, a crosspiece may be inserted directly in the split end as in Fig. 2A. When the branch splits far and there is little resilience, however, a crosspiece will wobble and fall out unless tied securely with straw or wire as in Fig. 2B.

If the crosspiece is either too thick or too thin it will not be very effective. It is best to use a piece whose diameter is about half that of the main branch, and split it in two.

3. The crossbar anchor (Fig. 3):

This is a technique often used in standing a branch upright. A support is cut to a length slightly less than the inside dimension of the vase and tied on in cruciform fashion in order to fix the branch in the desired position (see Fig. 3). As the ends of the supporting stick are braced against the sides of the vase, the branch cannot move sideways. When inserting this crossbar anchor through the mouth of the

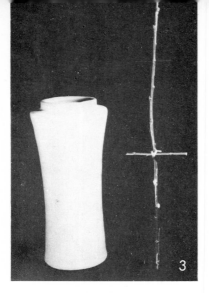

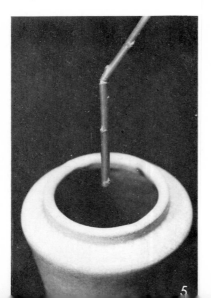

vase, the crosspiece is left loosely tied at an oblique angle; after it has passed the mouth of the vase, it is adjusted to a horizontal position and firmly tied with straw or string inside the vase.

At this time also it is imperative that the end of the branch stand firmly on the bottom of the vase in order to maintain upright stability.

4. Lengthwise splitting (Fig. 4):

When the branch is to be placed at a deep angle, or under conditions in which the methods explained in section 2 are unsuccessful, split the end of the branch and insert a support in the direction opposite to the angle of inclination. When the branch tends to split deeply, the support must be tied on securely with straw or wire.

The length of the support depends upon both the angle and length of the branch itself; but the longer it is, the more contact it has within the vase, increasing the force of resistance and thus the firmness of fixation.

5. Bending:

In addition to the above methods, the branch itself may be bent in order to contact the sides of the vase and thus hold it in place. This technique is generally used in the case of light branches and stemmed flowers which can be bent either upward or downward, according to the shape of the vase, in order to obtain support on the sides of the vase.

Fundamental Styles

The Essence of Moribana and Heika

The distinction between *moribana* and *heika* lies primarily in the difference in containers and flowers used.

A vase, i.e., a small-mouthed container with height and depth, indicates the *heika* style. In *moribana*, a flat, wide-mouthed, plate-shaped container is used. The *moribana* basin was first created by the originator of the *moribana* style, Unshin Ohara, founder of the Ohara School. This marked the end of "decorative" ikebana, for nature was taken to heart in redesigning this basin in which to "pile" flowers.

The *heika* style can be traced to the use of flowers in the tea ceremony, and to the way in which they were used by the painters and poets of the Edo period: the flowers used were those typical of the particular season, and this is still characteristic of the style. In addition, the materials must lend themselves to arrangement in a vase. *Moribana*, on the other hand, has a more universal character which enables it to embrace any and all kinds of flower materials.

One must take into consideration the special characteristics of the flower materials themselves in order not to lose the particular beauty inherent in each.

1

2

3

MORIBANA FORMS

UPRIGHT

The basic form of *moribana* is the Upright arrangement, and it is also the most popular form. Each branch serves to complement the others so that, viewed as a whole, the composition has an air of stability and calm.

Because the Subject (*Shu*) branch is placed, as illustrated, straight upright in the back left-hand side of the basin, the Upright form has been nicknamed the "Subject Placed Back" arrangement. The very uprightness of the Subject branch is, quite naturally, the outstanding characteristic of this form.

The Secondary (*Fuku*) branch is placed at an angle 45° from the vertical, and at an angle of 30° to the left of front if the arrangement is visualized in plan (i.e., from the top).

The Object (*Kaku*) branch is placed at an angle 60° from the vertical, and 45° right of front in plan, on the right-hand side of the basin.

23

SLANTING

For its Subject branches, this form uses curved branches and those which have grown naturally at an angle, and is thus called the Slanting form. Every position is nearly opposite its counterpart in the above-mentioned Upright form, so instead of "Subject Placed Back," it is nicknamed the "Subject Placed Forward" arrangement. The Subject is placed in the position of the Secondary of the Upright form, at an angle of 70° from the vertical, 45° to the left of front in plan. The Secondary is in exactly the same position as the Subject of the Upright Form, and the Object is 50° from the vertical, 30° to the right of front in plan.

24

1

2

3

CASCADE

Trailing vines like the wisteria or akebia, or similar flowers whose branches have been trained to grow on trellises, provide the main materials of this Cascade form. Because the tip of the Subject trails over and down, beyond the edge of the bowl, care should be taken to display this kind of arrangement in a location which will show it at its best. The Subject is placed at an angle 130° from the vertical, 45° to the left of front; the Secondary is exactly the same as in the Slanting form; and the Object is 45° from the vertical and 30° to the right of front in plan.

25

HEAVENLY

This form, while utilizing straight and erect flower materials, also is useful when one wishes to express strongly the upward-reaching quality inherent in these materials. The Subject is placed straight up in the center of the front portion of the basin, its length being 1.5 times the diameter of the container. Taking best advantage of the straight upward-reaching line formed by the Subject, the Secondary is to be within 30° both from the vertical and from the front in plan; the Object 80° from the vertical and within 30° of front in order to accent the line of the Subject as strongly as possible. Any intermediate branches must in all cases be cut shorter than the Secondary and arranged to emphasize the strength of the Subject.

26

CONTRASTING

The special characteristic of the Contrasting form is the balance of slanting branches and upright, as well as cascading flower materials, in a beautifully integrated composition.

The lengths of the principle branches are fixed, but the position of the Subject and Secondary branches are limited only by the 30° boundary forward and back from the line drawn parallel to the front through the base of the arrangement in plan. The angle from the vertical is left to the discretion of the arranger.

The Secondary is placed on the opposite side of the Subject in a position which balances and contrasts with it in a kind of symmetry. The Object is placed on the line of symmetry (i.e., center) between the Subject and the Secondary, at an angle of 80° from the vertical.

Heika Forms

UPRIGHT

When arranging in the Upright form, it is important to remember that because the shape of the Subject is tall and slender, one must be careful that the end of the Secondary does not extend so far to the left as to unbalance it. The Subject, according to our rule, stands straight up from the left forward position; but when viewed from the front, a slight pitch forward seems more natural, so it may be placed anywhere within a 15° angle from the vertical. The Secondary is at a 60° angle, 30° to left of center so that the part directly over the lip of the vase is exactly in line with the Subject when viewed from the front. The Object is positioned nearly dead center in the vase, 80° from the vertical.

28

SLANTING

The Slanting form is the basic form of *heika* arrangement. Branches are arranged to appear as if they were growing naturally, with the following design principals to serve as a guide: The Subject is placed at an angle of 45° to the left of front from a central position, 70° from the vertical. The Secondary stands vertically to the left of the Subject, while the Object faces the direction opposite that of the Subject at an angle of 30° from front and 60° from the vertical.

1

2

3

4

CASCADE

The special feature of the Cascade form, whether in *heika* or *moribana*, is that it uses the elegance of trailing vines and trellis-trained branches as a mode of expression. The Subject is 130° from vertical, and 45° to the left of center in plan; the Secondary is 30° to the right of center and 45° from the vertical. In both Cascade forms the materials are usually cut longer than the basic lengths in order to avoid the stiff appearance caused by short branches.

30

1

2

3

HEAVENLY

Being of the same upward-reaching character as their *moribana* counterparts, the principal branches of the *heika* Heavenly form are also arranged in the forward center position of the container. In this case, the branches are easily managed by utilizing the crossbar anchor technique to place them within the vase. The Subject (as in the Upright form) is placed within a 15° limit from vertical, and the secondary within a 30° limit both from the vertical and to the left. Although the variation within these limits is free in the cases of Subject and Secondary, the Object must be at an angle 80° from the vertical, though it may be within a 30° limit to the right.

CONTRASTING

As *heika* utilizes the same means of expression as *moribana* by balancing left and right, the Subject and the Secondary are placed to the left and right respectively of the front center of the container.

One thing to be especially careful of in this form is the tendency of the branches to bunch together. The Subject and Secondary should therefore be inserted so that their lower ends cross.

The only instruction regarding the Object is that it must be placed tilted towards you at an 80° angle. Other than that, it should be used so as to display the special characteristics of the materials involved.

32

Color Scheme Arrangements

◇ REALISTIC

小原豊雲

新春の花

FLOWERS OF EARLY SPRING　　　　　　　*by Hōun Ohara*

CONTAINER: unglazed earthenware vase
MATERIALS: Ilex　　　chrysanthemum　　　young pine

This arrangement, in its combination of materials, is a standard for all formal occasions, and one might call it a work of high character. The chrysanthemum, for instance, is a symbol of the Imperial household in Japan; the young pine, being an evergreen, represents immortality and is therefore commonly used at New Year's. Plants with red berries like the Ilex (a type of bittersweet), *senryō* (Chloranthus glaber), *manryō* (spear-flower), *nanten* (nandia) and *sankirai* (smilax) are all auspicious, for they symbolize the gaiety of special occasions.

While dignity is vital to this kind of arrangement, in this work the use of highly-colored plant materials is counterbalanced by the unglazed container, thus attaining a very calm and composed sense of harmony.

35

筑紫光漣

風の精

SYLPHIDES   *by Kōren Tsukushi*

CONTAINER: unglazed rope-marked pot
MATERIALS: pussy willow   king daffodil

Taking advantage of the long, reaching branches of the pussy willow, the Subject was deliberately left long in an attempt to exploit
the attraction of unbalance. However, to keep this one branch from
appearing to reach out too far alone, all the other members were also
tilted at the same angle as if to flow in rhythm with it. As to the selection of flowers, because the daffodil is usually very sweet, where a
more sweeping flower was desired, the giant blooms of the king
daffodil were employed to strengthen the design of this work.

36

平光波

鄙の家

RUSTIC COTTAGE   *by Kōha Taira*

CONTAINER: rice-vendor's small bamboo basket measure
MATERIALS: plum   white chrysanthemum

    The contrast of curving plum branches with the straight lines of
small branches is of particular interest as an ikebana effect, and it is best
to take advantage of these natural properties. The tiny white chrysanthemum used with the deep-pink plum blossoms display in a very
casual way the impression of spring in the mountains and fields. The
bamboo basket with its rustic flavor serves to enhance this ikebana of
soft and quiet nostalgia.

38

増子翠波

島影

SEASCAPE   *by Suiha Masuko*

CONTAINER: mottled glaze modern vase
MATERIALS: pine   camellia   spirea snow willow

Using the moss-covered trunk of a pine tree with its gently curving branches, this is a work of special character. The heavy strength
of the old pine is modified by the softness of transitory pale white
sprays of spirea. The solemn evergreens, camellia and pine, with
the softspoken elegance of the spirea, display a judicious sense of
harmony. The opened flowers of the camellia were pruned so that
the large blooms appear hidden among the branches, making it
not only an elegant work, but a showy one. This arrangement as a
whole evidences scrupulous care and thoughtful consideration.

40

41

増子翠波　ためらい

TO LINGER   *by Suiha Masuko*

CONTAINER: Turkish-blue, snail-patterned basin
MATERIALS: Japanese quince   lily   magnolia grandiflore

Without destroying the lines of the long, off-shooting twigs of the Japanese quince, yet obeying flower arrangement rules, this work is typical of the Realistic style. The white lily, placed high in the middle, is used before its bloom is fully open to avoid a distracting abruptness, with its petals still wrapped in the calyx. The Object flower is large and impressive. Flowers full of the colors of spring were selected to harmonize with the shapes of the branches. Especially noteworthy is the slanted, forward-projecting branch which balances perfectly the other flowers and leaves.

42

矛盾　児玉翠華

CONTRADICTION

by Suika Kodama

CONTAINER: blue modern vase

MATERIALS: magnolia liliflora   Itaya maple   trumpet lily

The pale green leaves of the Itaya maple are used here, and the crow magnolia branch was allowed to rise forward and upward in its natural curve. The upward-reaching branch, especially, is stripped of its small branches and soars high above, with one flower and one bud remaining aloft in space. So that the branches do not appear tall to the extent of being unreal, one more flower, the trumpet lily, was placed in their midst for color contrast.

44

45

小原豊雲　モザイク

MOSAIC   *by Hōun Ohara*

CONTAINER: footed freestyle basin

MATERIALS: Japanese quince   iris   camellia

The camellia placed low near the edge of the container and the iris used high are in keeping with the natural characteristics of these flowers; but in this case, the flowers of spring are treated in a coloristic fashion. We tried using flowers to fill in the spaces between leaves. As the camellia leaves and flowers are used extremely low, the character of the iris is that much more emphasized. One might call the space created by the composition of the extending branches of Japanese quince the main theme of this work. When arranging the iris as if in a natural environment, the leaves are not split apart from one another, but cut off (together) at the base and adjusted according to the height of the flower.

46

47

児
玉
翠
華

貿
易
風

TRADE WINDS   *by Suika Kodama*

CONTAINER: white-glazed freestyle vase
MATERIALS: anthurium   dracaena   Matteuccia fern

This is a simple work composed mainly of tropical plants. The striped configuration of the dracaena, with its leaves spreading boldly in all directions, is modulated sharply by the anthurium, whose shape and color seem almost unreal; both are integrated completely with the vase design. The fern seems to be placed very casually around the base of the dracaena, but as an accent it pulls the whole arrangement together.

48

五島泰雲
ローマの泉

ROMAN FOUNTAIN   *by Taiun Goshima*

CONTAINER: North African vase
MATERIALS: cosmos   wisteria vine   pampas grass

Conveying the clear, open feeling of autumn, this work has a delightfully refreshing quality. While cosmos is originally native to Central America, it is commonly seen blooming in Japan, from summer through autumn. It is so popular, in fact, that it is also referred to as "autumn cherry," countering the cherry of spring. Placed between the pure white pampas grass and the interesting winding lines of the wisteria vine, the long-stemmed cosmos are well distributed to provide the necessary balance. The old vase is also in excellent taste, complementing the arrangement well.

50

Color Scheme Arrangements

◇ NON-REALISTIC

魔 五
女 島
　 泰
　 雲

ENCHANTRESS   *by Taiun Goshima*

CONTAINER: unglazed modern vase
MATERIALS: daffodil leaves   lady's slipper

   Daffodil leaves, curved, twisted, and curled in various degrees and
shapes, are used in this arrangement. The leaves in the center are
curled to form almost full circles; the others, extending upward and
downward, are variously twisted and curved to avoid monotony in
their shapes. The conventional way of arranging daffodil leaves extending high upwards is to take advantage of their straight lines, but
here they were curled and twisted by drawing them through the finger-
tips to produce interesting forms. The leaves are extended so that their
lengths are approximately the height of the container, and a single
lady's slipper was placed at the base to hold down the extravagant flow
of the lines.

54

宇佐川豊俊

灯台

LIGHTHOUSE   *by Hōshun Usagama*

CONTAINER: goblet-shaped modern vase
MATERIALS: pine   rose   tridents

  The pine trunk extends strongly towards the front, and the green of
the mossy trunk and the pine needles are shown to full advantage, as are
the shapes of the roses. In the midst of these rather formal flower
materials, tridents were prominently displayed—upside-down. This
bold creation retains a surprisingly natural appearance, a harmony
provided in part by the shape of the modern-style container and its
chiseled pattern. A feeling of strength was gained by positioning the
materials firmly.

瓜生超

勝利

VICTORIA

by Chō Uryū

CONTAINER: variegated glazed modern vase

MATERIALS: erica   calla lily   sweet pea   maidenhair fern

This work seems to have much in common in feeling with the flower decoration of Western countries, but it is managed according to ikebana techniques. It is true that ikebana is usually viewed only from the front, but this does not mean it should appear in only two dimensions: it must also have "depth," even in the case of Non-realistic arrangements. The branches of erica extend downward in front, with the calla and maidenhair fern accenting the right-hand side display, harmonizing with the space created by the slanting erica.

59

オアシス　　宇佐川豊俊

OASIS   *by Hōshun Usagawa*

CONTAINER: white-glazed, footed container
MATERIAL: sansevieria   Kaffir lily   asparagus fern
   On the left-hand side the mottled leaves of the sansevieria were rolled
under in order to balance the mass of asparagus fern on the right-hand
side. As the sansevieria leaves are mottled white on both sides, rolling
greatly increases their effect. The Kaffir lilies are placed casually, but in
order to balance and solidify the lines to left and right, great care was
taken in deciding their size and height.

螺旋　　大貫文男

HELIX   *by Fumio Ōnuki*

CONTAINER: unglazed modern vase
MATERIALS: pussy willow   calla lilies   begonia

In unified color scheme, the main material, pussy willow, is given strength by Non-realistic techniques. The long branches of the pussy willow were formed in circular fashion, aiming at the beauty of space formed by such lines; the fuzzy white buds serve to accent the curving branches. The calla lilies also are not left in their natural state, for the petals were bent from the middle outward, exposing the centers in a rather different and unusual form.

62

63

砂 大
の 貫
丘 文
　 男

DUNES   *by Fumio Ōnuki*

CONTAINER: white-glazed freestyle vase
MATERIALS: skunk cabbage   century plant (agave)   bleached broom
  In Japan, the skunk cabbage is seen only in the remote, cold and
swampy areas of the country, and large specimens are unusual. The
skunk cabbage is called in Japanese "the grass that grows in the shape
of a Buddhist priest sitting in meditation"; the strangeness of its form,
combined with the spiny-leaved century plant, provides an interesting
composition. The bleached broom swirls around the skunk cabbage
and completely removes it from its natural environment, transforming
the overall image into a botanic fantasy of the dunes.

64

65

大貝豊春
人魚

MERMAID   *by   Hōshun   Ōgai*

CONTAINER: freestyle compote
MATERIALS: cymbidium   dracaena   trident (branches)
   By placing the bare white trident branches invertedly, a change of
form creates interest in the midst of color. While the deep-colored dracaena leaves accentuate the tridents, opening wheel-fashion in all
directions, the gregarious cymbidium flowers are used both tall and
forward, aiming at a sumptuous effect. Although the cymbidium
and dracaena are used in natural fashion, the inclusion of tridents
removes this ikebana from the world of realism.

小原豊雲

秋の祭り

AUTUMN FESTIVAL   *by Hōun Ohara*

CONTAINER: stoneware freestyle vase
MATERIALS: fox face   cockscomb   pampas grass

Using the unusual shape of the vase as a starting point, the strong contrast of pure red and yellow is designed to bring out the festive feeling of autumn. Although the surprised fox-face shapes create the mood of a fable, this work is not intended as a pictorial description, but is inspired rather by the nostalgic memories of a childhood festival long ago.

Inasmuch as the technique is somewhat contrived—the cockscomb used in masses and the pampas grass being in an unnatural state— this is termed a non-real ikebana.

旋　工
律　藤
　　和
　　彦

COUNTERPOINT   *by Kazuhiko Kudō*

CONTAINER: green-glazed vase
MATERIALS: Scotch broom   anthurium   asparagus fern
　　　　　　bleached mountain fern

 The numerous small branches of the Scotch broom are bent and
coiled in toward the center. The thick main stems and the lines of their
offshoots are also curved in a snail-shaped pattern. Each of the bleached mountain ferns is also coiled, but toward the outside so as to expose
the white flowers in contrast with the Scotch broom. The anthurium
flowers are inserted upside down to emphasize the non-realistic feeling
of the composition. The lines of the Scotch broom, contrasting with
the mass of mountain fern, plus the juxtaposition of red, white, and
green, constitute the main theme of this arrangement.

70

金子三伸

異国のひと

DELEILA   *by Sanshin Kaneko*

CONTAINER: white-glazed freestyle vase
MATERIALS: coconut palm   alocasia   anthurium

The aim of this composition is to obtain a harmony between the palm and the container. The arrangement seems simple, but an excellent balance of strength is maintained between the space created by the palm placed high upright, the cross-shaped container placed at an angle, and the palm extending horizontally. The alocasia and anthurium are inserted so as to cut through the spaces created by the concave curves of the palm and to form a movement in the same direction. The white veins of the alocasia emphasize this line of movement to the upper left to complete the composition, an expression of simplicity and strength.

72

73

金子三伸

祭り

FESTIVAL   *by Sanshin Kaneko*

CONTAINER: freestyle vase
MATERIALS: green bamboo   bird-of-paradise   dried reed

   Pieces of green bamboo were split and fitted into one another to
make a frame and provide form. Dried reeds, bent and tied into the
shapes of bursting stars, were then fastened to the bamboo. The long
line on the right-hand side is balanced by the volume of the form on the
left, with strong accent added by the radiating lines of the reddish-
brown reed. Looking as if it were bursting out of its calyx, the exotic
bird-of-paradise carries an upward-reaching vitality against the strong
horizontal feeling. The colors are subdued, but are more than compen-
sated for by the power of the overall form. It seems to bring to mind
the image of fireworks at a festival.

74

75

Landscape Arrangements

◇ TRADITIONAL

清　平
浄　光
　　波

INNOCENCE   *by Kōha Taira*

CONTAINER: Turkish-blue, snail-patterned basin
MATERIALS: pussy willow   violet orchid   club moss
　　In both the selection of flowers and the way of placing them,
this is a typical Traditional arrangement for spring.　These pussy
willow shapes of early spring, blooming white fuzzy buds, are bunched
together at the bottom and inserted as one clump, like a single tree
standing by the edge of a pond, at the base of which a small flower
blooms. The artist's eye told him to place slightly larger blooms of
this same flower to the near right in order to evoke the feeling of perspective. Because it is a spring of moving water, the basin was left
one-third full, the container itself being selected for its sculptured
ripples. The air of an innocent spring morning is expressed.

78

尾田光秋
こだま

ECHO   *by Kōshū Oda*

CONTAINER: blue round basin
MATERIALS: dragon willow   iris   standing club moss

   This is a distant landscape expressed in ikebana. The un-ryu
willow is placed — one heavy branch in the center with smaller
branches inserted around it as if it were a single tree standing
by the water's edge. The iris appears to be growing in a pool, with
a large expanse of water around it, and the leaves of the iris are placed
as they would be in reality. As iris blooms from the beginning of
spring through late fall, there are many ways of arranging it as the
seasons pass; here, the leaves of spring are shown small to indicate
that they are not yet full-grown.

80

Landscape Arrangements

◇ INTERPRETIVE

前奏曲　　泉谷豊宣

PRELUDE   *by Hōsen Izutani*

CONTAINER: stoneware compote
MATERIALS: Japanese quince   summer cypress   wall iris

The leaves of the wall iris are usually readjusted to bring out their beauty in a more obvious way, but they were arranged here as if in two natural clumps. Therefore this arrangement does not adhere to the formal principle of "leaf arrangement" (*hagumi*), in which the length and facing of the leaves are fixed: it is left entirely to the creativity of the artist. The quince near water level stretches its branches as if whispering to the waters of spring. Summer cypress is used to depict a mountain scene, while at the same time its tiny red-orange buds deepen the feeling of spring.

85

山路のほとり　　松本豊水

BY THE MOUNTAIN PATH   *by Hōsui Matsumoto*

CONTAINER: fan-shaped freestyle basin

MATERIALS: Japanese quince   Japanese iris   dried reed

This example of a landscape reproduced in ikebana is not merely
an attempt to arrange flowers beautifully; it must express a landscape
as it might actually appear in its natural state. It seeks to capture a
rustic beauty—a wild beauty we might find while walking through
wood and field. A jumbled bit of nature that would usually go unno-
ticed catches our attention, and we are charmed. The key to this arrangement lies in the use of dried reed and Japanese iris: if the arrangement is done in a random and haphazard manner, it will simply appear
unkempt, a far cry from true rustic flavor. This, in essence, is a sketch
of a mountain path in early spring.

金
森
光
堂

深
淵
の
唄

SONG OF DEEP WATERS   *by Kōdō Kanamori*

CONTAINER: black-glazed, leaf-shaped basin
MATERIALS: camellia flowers   iris   moss-covered branch

This is a scene of early spring at the water's edge. The mossy branch
laid sideways, skillfully using the Spanish moss with the iris left in its
natural formation, creates the scene of a floating island in a lake or
beside a seaweed-lined shore. To emphasize early spring, groups of
two small iris leaves are used low, and one bloom only of the iris,
usually seen high, is cut short and placed in a very low position. On
the surface of the water to the left are scattered the flowers of the
winter-blooming camellia, having fallen far upstream, flowing and
flowing until they made their way to this spot, where spring has
already come. In this way, the change of the seasons is expressed in a
subtle, yet highly effective, way.

88

89

木陰のささやき　金森光堂

UNDER WHISPERING BOUGHS   *by Kōdō Kanamori*

CONTAINER: unglazed, three-footed basin
MATERIALS: small pine   brocade   red azalea   royal fern
            aster   dried bulrush

In contrast to the depiction of a distant forest, depicting a landscape
that is close at hand involves showing the natural characteristics of
individual plants in order to gain a truly realistic effect. This is an
important principle. In other words, it is the technique of magnifying
the small flowers found beneath trees. These tiny flowers create a happy
feeling, indeed a brilliant work overflowing with the mood of spring
time.

91

尾田光秋

風焰

WIND-FLAME   *by Kōshū Oda*

CONTAINER: freestyle modern vase
MATERIALS: cherry branch   red vine   Japanese pampas
               Matteuccia fern   mountain fern

The wind howls through a mountain gorge. The cherry and pampas
blooming on the precipice are blown all in one direction with the flow
of the wind, making one sense the feeling of such a wind-traversed
world. Bringing out movement in the flowers themselves, a rhythmical
pulse opens out from within the limits of the framework that is the
container. The red vine, as well as helping to depict a mountain
fastness, brings a change within the flower formation, which, as a
whole, moves in one direction. The mountain fern placed as an under-
grass helps complete the atmosphere of nature in the abundant spring-
time.

92

泉谷豊宣

森の朝

FOREST MORNING   *by Hōsen Izutani*

CONTAINER: yellow-seto ware rectangular basin
MATERIALS: *uriwa* maple   mossy defoliated pine   calla lily

The old pine tree trunk offset to one side gives one the impression of deep forest; in this forest, Spanish moss is entwined to convey mist. The small budding maple branches are arranged as refreshingly as the traces of a morning breeze. Only the blooms of the calla lily were used because, although in reality they would never appear in such a setting, they are meant in their pure whiteness and large-petaled form to represent, momentarily, the general image of new plants just making their way into the world. A freshness appropriate to the theme of morning is expressed in the Landscape manner.

94

尾田光秋

野と丘

HILLS AND MEADOWS   *by Kōshū Oda*

CONTAINER: two-mouthed freestyle container
MATERIALS: weeping mulberry   Japanese iris   small pine
          Itaya maple thistle
   In keeping with the freestyle vase, the mulberry branches bring out
the flavor of the outdoors, and special attention was given the treat-
ment of the iris leaves. In reality, a thistle would not be taller than a
small pine or mulberry, but by making this small flower seem tall,
the depth of scenic expression is increased and the strong growing
quality of field grasses emphasized. It is indeed a true fiction. The
branches of the mulberry, if arranged upright, would not make a scenic
composition; the beauty of hills and meadows is thus suggested by
artificial variation.

96

五　城
島　の
泰　濠
雲

CASTLE MOAT   *by Taiun Goshima*

CONTAINER: striped modern style vase
MATERIALS: lotus flower   seed pods   dried leaves

    The lotus is a material which can be used in many ways from the beginning of summer until late autumn. In the depths of autumn, however, the large leaves of the lotus, once high above the water, dry and become colored in their forlorn existence. The seed-pods contribute to this desolate scene. A single, lingering bloom continues to live among the nearly lifeless leaves. That a blossom should still exist among dried seed-pods seems unnatural; but here, because of this very flower, the feeling of the dead leaves is emphasized. This might be called an ikebana fiction.

98

Rimpa (Classical Painting School) Tone Arrangements

「かきつばた屏風」に寄せて　小原豊雲

FROM "THE IRIS SCREEN" *by Hōun Ohara*

CONTAINER: red clay rectangular basin

MATERIALS: Japanese iris philadelphus

    This work was inspired by the folding-screen painting "Iris" by Kōrin. Although it uses the *hagumi* (artificial leaf arrangement) technique, and can therefore be considered a formal arrangement, the stalks of the iris are actually arranged in a bold *shizengumi* (natural) fashion. The strong vertical line of the iris, counterbalanced by the gently *curving* philadelphus, compose a work of highly decorative qualities.

102

小原豊雲

華麗な春

A SPLENDID SPRING   *by Hōun Ohara*

CONTAINER: Chinese handled basket
MATERIALS: peony   thistle   hydrangea   Solomon's seal
            Japanese pampas

    This work, rather than utilizing the patterns suggested by the natural plant shapes, is arranged in a thoroughly decorative manner. It conveys the same impression as the folding screen paintings of "Flower and Grass" themes by the Rimpa school. The mottled leaves of the Solomon's seal have a highly decorative impact, while the hydrangea is more subdued; with the addition of flowers like the peony, a gay and brightly colored ikebana is the result.

104

105

梅
雨
の
あ
と

小
原
豊
雲

AFTER THE RAINY SEASON   *by Hōun Ohara*

CONTAINER: rectangular basin by the second generation master of
        the Ohara School.
MATERIALS: bamboo shoot   hydrangea   azalea   Polystichum
        fern   red starlily

This work is an expression of characteristic natural plant patterns.
The strong, viable accent of the fat bamboo shoot is used to its best
advantage, while the inflourescent hydrangea surrounded by leaves
can be considered a kind of crest. While the vertical line of the bamboo
alone would become monotonous spatially, the horizontality of the
Polystichum fern counterbalances the composition. The azalea and
the lily both add a decorative effect to the arrangement.

Both materials and form are in accordance with the Rimpa taste as
shown in the "Flower and Grass" paintings of the Rimpa school.

106

Bunjin (Literary Artist) Tone Arrangements

初夏の語らい　　小原豊雲

A TALE OF EARLY SUMMER　　　　　　*by Hōun Ohara*

CONTAINER: freestyle, green-glazed bowl
MATERIALS: Sagittaria　　loquat　　chrysanthemum
   This work in the Bunjin Tone style takes the shapes of the first
flowers of summer just as they are, placing the strong leaf of the Sagittaria high above the interesting branch formation of the loquat and the
fragile chrysanthemum without any particular technique. These three
characters so casually arranged seem to be engaged in a conversation
by the seaside.

110

111

竹林の瞑想　小原豊雲

BAMBOO GROVE CONTEMPLATION   *by Hōun Ohara*

CONTAINER: Chinese-style vase
MATERIALS: arrow bamboo   cactus   chrysanthemum

In actuality, there is no such thing as the combination of bamboo and cactus in China. If exoticism was synonymous with Chinese in the Edo period, modern ikebana prefers adapting the spirit of Bunjin to new materials and combinations in order to open new frontiers; this work is a good example of this trend.

Upon beholding the strange shape of the cactus beneath the tall arrow bamboo, one is apt to be reminded of a hermit taking a stroll. In Chinese the character for cactus is written as "the palm of the hermit," so this association may not be purely accidental.

112

113

小原豊雲

実のころ

THE TIME OF FRUIT   *by Hōun Ohara*

CONTAINER: green-glazed compote
MATERIALS: pomegranate   cockscomb   tiny chrysanthemum

    The fruits of autumn may almost always be used in Bunjin Tone arrangements; but among these, the pomegranate bears an especially propitious meaning, for its character is written as "many children." If carried out in the true Chinese fashion, a miscanthus reed would have been used, but here the neat white chrysanthemum is used instead. The inflorescent cockscomb used in masses expresses an auspicious autumn harvest.

114

Shohinka (Small Flower Arrangements)

崖 工
の 藤
花 和
　 彦

FROM A MOUNTAIN CREVICE   *by Kazuhiko Kudō*

CONTAINER: unglazed compote
MATERIALS: amaryllis   young pine   gingko tree branches

　Above the gingko branches which cross and embrace the tufts of young pine, the flower of the amaryllis is displayed prominently. A very casual arrangement, some of the new sprouts on the branches were left as they were to harmonize with the texture of the container. By severely limiting the choice of material, both in amount and in variety, and then applying the abbreviated technique required for *shohinka*, emphasis is given to the freshness and originality of the selection. Unexpectedly discovering the beauty of one single bloom on an otherwise barren trellis—is this not the kind of feeling evoked?

118

119

胡蝶の精のおどり　　筑紫光漣

ELFIN DANCE　　　　　　　　　　　　*by Kōren Tsukushi*

CONTAINER: freestyle vase
MATERIALS: spice bush　　Orchis rupestris

   The orchids were placed in a small red container to create an impressionistic *shohinka* arrangement. As the Orchis rupestris is called "butterfly orchid" in Japanese, the spice bush branches were used long in order to emphasize the dancing quality of butterflies. The blooms scattered here and there seem to be the buzzing of wings, the three-winged hum of butterfly forms. The reason for such random use of the orchids is that in such a small container as this, the arrangement would otherwise tend to be unstable. The contrast of the pure white shapes of these clustered flower-butterflies with the scattered yellow blooms of the spice bush is the main theme of this work.

120

工藤和彦
まどろみ

DAYDREAM   *by Kazuhiko Kudō*

CONTAINER: colored glass vase
MATERIALS: mulberry vine   dried sunflower   red and white camellias

The colors of the flower materials seem to have succeeded in matching the coloration in the glass vase. The wiggling line of the vine reaches high, the dried sunflower catching the mood of a child's painting, while the red and white camellias too are treated so as to create a joyful *shohinka* arrangement. The dried sunflower often provokes a feeling of wierdness, but its color scheme is integrated to evoke a joyful feeling instead.

122

123

工　フ
藤　ラ
和　ミ
彦　ン
　　ゴ

FLAMINGO   *by Kazuhiko Kudō*

CONTАINER: glass vase
MATERIALS: Orchis rupestris   young pine   ostrich plume
   Because a *shohinka* arrangement involves so few flowers, it is most
important to select them carefully, and equally as crucial to choose the
right container for them. These flower materials were chosen to cele-
brate the autumn equinox. In the Ohara School, the combined use of
native Japanese flowers and imported varieties is normally considered
as conflicting with a sense of naturalness, but in this small freestyle
arrangement, the visual impact of color and form is more important
than the natural properties of the flowers. At any rate, the overall
effect of the exotic ostrich plume and "butterfly" orchid, combined with
the young pine often found in Japanese ceremonial arrangements, is
not really unnatural. In this slender-necked glass vase, the tiny orchids
were intended to create the elegant impression of a flamingo by the sea.

124

平　か
光　ま
波　き
　　り

MANTIS   *by Kōha Taira*

CONTAINER: cobalt underglaze, decorated Korean vase
MATERIALS: dried reed   camellia

    Just one dried reed, and one flower on a camellia branch. Using only these simple materials, a rigid spatial composition and the beauty of ikebana display is attained. Though it is called a *shohinka*, this arrangement is closer to that used in a teahouse, from the standpoint of the outwardly simple treatment given it. It is like arranging a plain field flower as if it were growing in a field, but providing it with a fresh beauty and lyricism that goes straight to our hearts. Had dozens of camellia blossoms been used, their colorful beauty would, of course, have captivated the eye, but here an attempt has been made to create an impression of ever-widening space through the angle formed by only a single branch, a single blossom.

126

秋 小
の 原
愁 豊
い 雲

AUTUMN LAMENT   *by   Hōun   Ohara*

CONTAINER: gunmetal-glazed vase (saké-bottle shape)
MATERIALS: jack bean   giant knotweed   clematis
   Although nut-bearing materials are representative of autumn, it is
usually trees that come to mind, rather than grass. In this case,
the wild jack bean emphasizes with its elegant curves the beauty
of its seeds dropped down low; the flower of the giant knotweed
evokes the feeling of the season. In accordance with the purple hue of
the modest clematis, the color tone is uniform and the damp softness
of the flowers seems to tell of the quiet lamenting of autumn.

128

Diagrams of Basic Styles

DIAGRAM OF THE OHARA SCHOOL'S BASIC MORIBANA STYLES

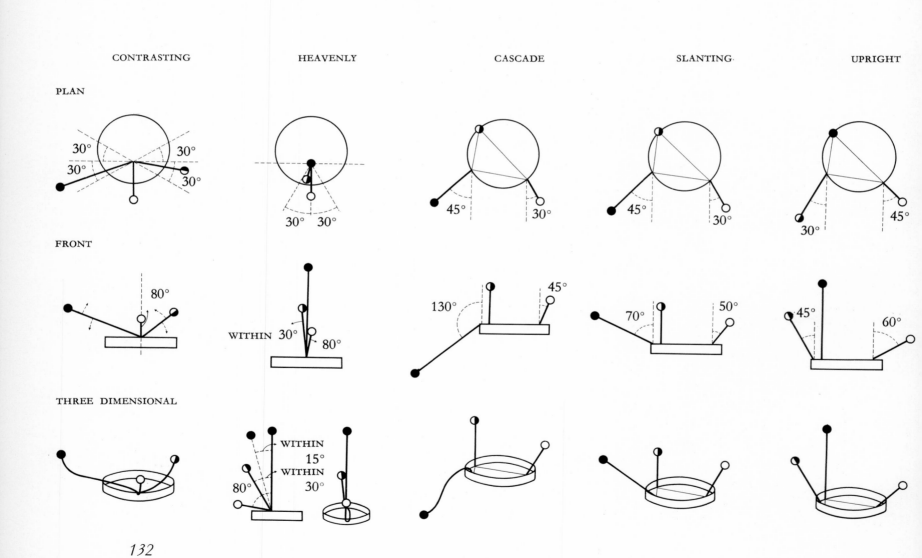

CONTRASTING   HEAVENLY   CASCADE   SLANTING   UPRIGHT

PLAN

FRONT

THREE DIMENSIONAL

DIAGRAM OF THE OHARA SCHOOL'S BASIC HEIKA STYLES

● SUBJECT
◖ SECONDARY
○ OBJECT

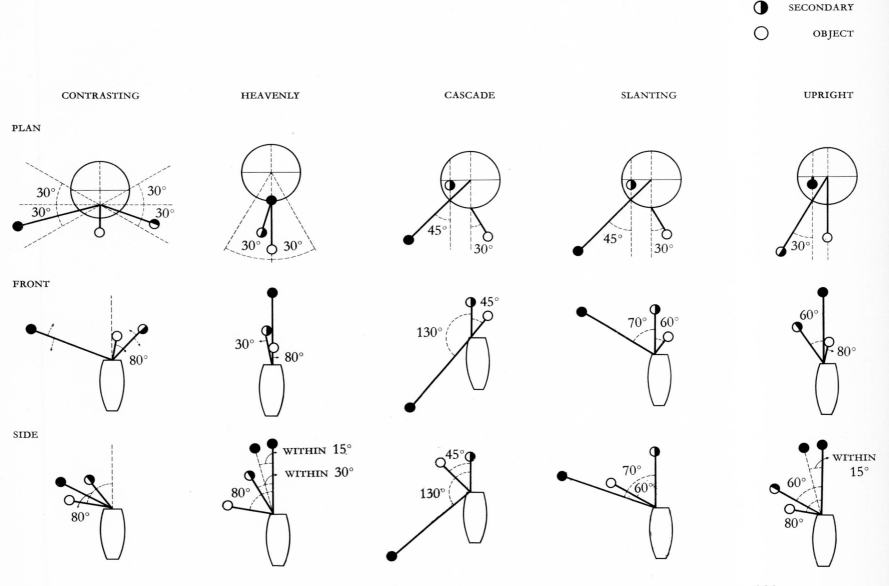

	CONTRASTING	HEAVENLY	CASCADE	SLANTING	UPRIGHT
PLAN					
FRONT					
SIDE					